Nazokat Rustamova
Farangiz Negmatova

World of Fairy tales

Nazokat Rustamova
Farangiz Negmatova

World of Fairy tales

with exercises

JustFiction Edition

Imprint

Any brand names and product names mentioned in this book are subject to trademark, brand or patent protection and are trademarks or registered trademarks of their respective holders. The use of brand names, product names, common names, trade names, product descriptions etc. even without a particular marking in this work is in no way to be construed to mean that such names may be regarded as unrestricted in respect of trademark and brand protection legislation and could thus be used by anyone.

Cover image: www.ingimage.com

Publisher:
JustFiction! Edition
is a trademark of
Dodo Books Indian Ocean Ltd., member of the OmniScriptum S.R.L Publishing group
str. A.Russo 15, of. 61, Chisinau-2068, Republic of Moldova Europe
Printed at: see last page
ISBN: 978-620-3-57666-5

Authors: Rustamova Nazokat

Negmatova Farangiz

Reviewers:

Yusupov Otabek - The dean of English faculty II

Zubaydova Nilufar– teacher in English faculty II

***

"Fairy tales are more than true: not because they tell us that dragons exist, but because they tell us that dragons can be beaten."
— **Neil Gaiman, <u>Coraline</u>**

***

"If you want your children to be intelligent, read them fairy tales. If you want them to be more intelligent, read them more fairy tales."
— **Albert Einstein**

***

"When I was a little girl I used to read fairy tales. In fairy tales you meet Prince Charming and he's everything you ever wanted. In fairy tales the bad guy is very easy to spot. The bad guy is always wearing a black cape so you always know who he is. Then you grow up and you realize that Prince Charming is not as easy to find as you thought. You realize the bad guy is not wearing a black cape and he's not easy to spot; he's really funny, and he makes you laugh, and he has perfect hair."
— **Taylor Swift**

Preface

The teacher's fundamental task is to get students to engage in
learning process that are likely to result in achieving outcomes.
It is helpful to remember that what the student does is actually
more important that what the teacher does. Useful and funny little fairy tales are
ones where the student is able to take what they
have learnt from the language. In this book given fairy tales for all sorts of little
children. The pupil can learn useful information from the fairy tales and learn
English quickly and useful by doing various exercises given at the end of the fairy
tales.

The exercises are designed differently to increase pupils' grammar skill and
vocabulary source. Authors pay high attention to avoid sameness. A variety of
poems and fun games are provided to keep the reader from getting bored and
not to monotony during the exercises and reading the story. The poems at the
end of the tale are also given so as not to bore the child in the same way.

Content

WHY THE SUN AND THE MOON LIVE IN THE SKY

Many years ago, the sun and water were great friends, and they both lived on the Earth together. The Sun very often used to visit the water, but the water never returned the visits. At last the sun asked the water why he never visited. The water replied that the Sun`s house was not big enough, and that if he came with all his people, he would drive the Sun out of his home.

The water then said, "If you want me to visit you, you will have to build a very large house. But I warn you that it will have to be very large, as my people are numerous and take up a lot of room".

The Sun promised to build a very large house, and soon afterwards, he returned home to his wife, the Moon, who greeted him with a broad smile. The Sun told the Moon what he had promised the water, and the next day, they began building a large house to entertain the water and all his people. When it was completed, the Sun asked the water to come and visit him.

When the water arrived, one of his people called out to the Sun, and asked him whether it would be safe for the water to enter, and the Sun answered, "Yes, tell my friend to come in".

The water began to flow in, followed by the fish and all other water animals. Very soon, the water was knee-deep in the house, so he asked the Sun if it was still safe, and the Sun again said, "Yes", so more of them came in.

When the water at the level of a man`s head, the water said to the Sun,

"Do you want more of my people to come?"

 No knowing any better, the Sun and the Moon both said, "Yes". More and more of the water`s people came in, until the Sun and the Moon had to sit on top of the roof.

The water once again asked the Sun if it was still okay to keep coming in. The Sun and the Moon answered yes, so more and more of the water`s people came in. The water soon overflowed the top of the roof, and the Sun and the Moon were forced to go up into the sky.

… and they have been there ever since.

VOCABULARY

Both- har ikkisi

Return – qaytib kelmoq

Never- hech qachon

Replied – javob bermoq

Enough – yetarli

To warn – ogohlantirmoq

Numerous – ko`p sonli

To take up – egallamoq

To promise – va`da bermoq

Afterwards – keyin , so`ngra

A broad smile mayin tabassum

Entertain – ko`nglini ochmoq

Safe – xavfsiz

Overflowed – toshib ketmoq

FRIENDSHIP

Friends smile at you.
They like your face.
They want to be with you
Any old place.

Friends have fun with you.
Friends share
They are glad when you are happy-
When you`re sad, they care.

If you are a friend

Then you care, too

That`s why your friends

Are glad you`re you!!!

It`s nice to have a friend like you!

I`ll tell you what I`m going to do.

Because you make me so fine.

PROVERBS

Old friends and old wine are best.

(Eski do`stlar va eski sharob eng yaxshisidir)

A friend to all is a friend of none

(Hammaga do`st hech kimga do`st emas)

A man is known by the company he keeps

(Insonning kimligi uning do`stlaridan bilinar)

A friend is never known till needed

(Do`stning o`rni kerak bo`lguncha hech qachon bilinmas)

Books and friends should be few, but good

(Kitoblar va do`stlar kam, ammo yaxshi bo`lishi kerak)

Count your age with friends but not with years

(Umringni yashagan yillaring bilan emas, do`stlaring bilan hisobla)

THE MAN WHO NEVER LIED

(AN AFRICAN FOLKTALE)

Once upon a time, there lived a wise man by the name of Mamad. He never lied. All the people in the land, even the ones who lived twenty days away, knew about him.

The king heard about Mamad and ordered his subjects to bring him to the place. He looked at the wise man and asked:

"Mamad, is it true, that you have never lied?"

"It is true".

"And you will never lie in your life?"

"I`m sure in that".

"Okay, tell the truth, but be careful!" The life is cunning and it gets on your tongue easily".

Several days passed and the king called Mamad once again. There was a big crowd: the king was about to go hunting. The king held his horse by the mane, his left foot was already on the stirrup. He ordered Mamad:

"Go to my summer palace and tell the queen I will be with her for lunch. Tell her to prepare a big feast. You will have lunch with me then".

Mamad bowed down and went to the queen. Then the king laughed and said:

"We won`t go hunting and now Mamad will lie to the queen. Tomorrow we will laugh on his behalf".

But the wise Mamad went to the palace and said:

"Maybe you should prepare a big feast for lunch tomorrow, and maybe you shouldn`t. Maybe the king will come by noon, and maybe he won`t."

"Tell me will he come, or won`t he?", - asked the queen.

"I don`t know weather, he put his right foot on the stirrup, or he put his left foot on the ground after I left".

Everybody waited for the king. He came the next day and said to the queen:

"The wise Mamad, who never lies, lied to you yesterday".

But the queen told him about the words of Mamad. And the king realized, that the wise man never lies, and says only that, which he saw with his own eyes.

(HANS ANDERSEN`S FAIRY TALES)

VOCABULARY

A wise man- dono odam

Truth – haqiqat, rost

Be careful- ehtiyot bo`lmoq

Cunning - makkorlik

Crowd – olomon

Held – o`tkazmoq

Mane – yol

Stirrup – uzangi

Feast – ziyofat

Bowed down – ta`zim qilmoq

TELL THE TRUTH

Tell all the Truth but tell it slant-
Success in Circuit lies
Too bright for our infirm Delight
The Truth`s superb surprise.

As Lighting to the Children eased
With explanation kind

The Truth must dazzle gradually

Or every man be blind.

PROVERBS

When money speaks, the truth keeps silent

(Pul gapirganda haqiqat sukut saqlaydi)

The Truth is a heavy burden that few care to carry

(Haqiqat bu shunday og`ir yukki , uni har kim ham ko`tara olmaydi)

Better suffer for the Truth than proper in a falsehood

(Yolg`ondan ko`ra haq uchun azonlanish yaxshiroqdir)

Truth fears nothing but concealment

(Haqiqat yashirinishdan boshqa hech narsadan qo`rqmaydi)

THE RED AND BLUE COAT

(AFRICAN FOLKTALE)

Once there were two boys who were great friends, and they were determined to remain that way forever. When they grew up and got married, they built their houses facing one another. There was a small path that formed a border between their farms.

One day, a trickster from the village decided to play a trick on them. He dressed himself in a two-color coat was divided down the middle. So, one side of the coat was red, and the other side was blue.

The trickster wore this coat and walked along the narrow path between the houses of the two friends. They were each working opposite each other in their fields. The trickster made enough noise as he passed them to make sure that each of them would look up and see him passing.

At the end of the day, one friend said to the other, "Wasn`t that a beautiful red coat that man was wearing today?"

"No", the other replied. "It was a blue coat".

"I saw the man clearly as he walked between us!" said the first, "His coat was red".

"You are wrong!" said the other man, "I saw it too, and it was blue".

"I know what I saw!" insisted the first man. "The coat was red!"

"You don`t know anything", the second man replied angrily. "It was blue!"

They kept arguing about this over and over, insulted each other, and eventually, they began to beat each other and roll around on the ground.

Just then, trickster returned and faced the two men, who were punching and kicking each other and shouting, "Our friendship is OVER!"

The tricksters walked directly in front of them, and showed them his coat. He laughed at their silly fight. The two friends saw this his coat was red on one side and blue on the other.

The two friends stopped fighting and screamed at the trickster saying, "We have lived side by side like brothers all our lives, and it is all your fault that we fighting. You have started a war between us".

"Don`t blame me for the battle", replied the trickster. "I did not make you fight. Both of you are wrong, and both of you are right. Yes, what each one saw was true.

You are fighting because you only looked at my coat from on your own point of view".

(HANS ANDERSEN`S FAIRY TALES)

VOCABULARY

Determined – dadil, qat`iy

Forever – abadiy

Got married – oila qurmoq

Border – chegara

A trickster – yolg`onchi

Divided – bo`linmoq

Side – tomon

Narrow – tor

Opposite – qarama- qarshi

Noise – shovqin

Clearly – aniq

Insisted -qattiq turib olmoq

Anything – hech narsa

Arguing – ta`kidlamoq

Punching – mushtlashmoq

Kicking – tepmoq

Shouting – baqirmoq

Directly – to`g`ri

Fighting – urushmoq

A COAT

I made my song a coat

Covered with embroideries

Out of old mythologies

From heel to throat;

But the fools caught it,

Wore it in the world's eyes

As though they'd wrought it.

Song, let them take it,

For there's more enterprise

In walked naked.

PROVERBS

A smart coat is a good letter

(Aqlli palto – bu tanishish uchun yaxshi xat)

Don't put golden buttons on a torn coat

(Yirtilgan paltoga oltin tugmachalarni qadama)

The forest is the poor man's overcoat

(O'rmon kambag'al odamning paltosi)

Under a ragged coat lies wisdom

(Yirtiq palto ostida donolik yotadi)

A borrowed coat does not keep one warm

(Qarzga olingan palto issiqni ushlab turmaydi)

Do not measure another man`s coat on your body
(Tanangizga boshqaning paltosini o`lchamang)

The wolf changes only his coat not his character
(Bo`ri faqatgina paltosini almashtiradi, xarakterini emas)

Do not judge by appearances, a rich heart may be under a poor coat
(Tashqi ko`rinishga baho berma eski palto ostida boy yurak joylashgan bo`lishi mumkin)

Never watch a bonfire wearing a straw coat
(Hech qachon somon palto kiyib gulxanni tomosha qilma)

The coat is quite new, only the holes are old
(Palto yangi bo`lgani bilan teshiklari eskiligicha qolaveradi)

If you add to the truth, you take something away from it
(Agar haqiqat bilan bo`lsang , undan ko`p narsa olasan)

Simplicity is the seal of the truth
(Oddiylik haqiqatning muhridir)

Sooner or later the truth will come to light
(Ertami- kechmi haqiqat yuzaga chiqadi)

THE GOLDEN BEETLE OR WHY THE DOG HATES THE CATS

(CHINESE FOLKTALE)

What we shall eat tomorrow, I haven`t the slightest idea!", said Widow Wang to her eldest son, as he started out one morning in search of work.

"Oh, the Gods will provide. I`ll find a few coppers somewhere", replied the boy, trying to speak cheerfully, although in his heart he also had not the slightest idea in which direction to turn.

The winter had been a hard one: extreme cold, deep snow, and violent winds. The Wang house had suffered greatly. The roof had fallen in, weighed down by heavy snow. Then a hurricane had blown a wall over, and Ming-li, the son, up all night and exposed to a bitter cold wind, had caught pneumonia. Long days of illness followed, with the spending of extra money for medicine. All their scant savings had soon melted and at the shop where Ming-li had been employed his place was filled by another. When at last he arose from his sickbed he was too weak for hard labor and there seemed to be no work in the neighboring villages for him to do. Night after night he came home, trying not to be discouraged, but in his heart feeling the deep pangs of sorrow that come to the good son who sees his mother suffering for want of food and clothing.

"Bless his good heart!", said the poor widow after he had gone. "No mother ever had a better boy. I hope he is right in saying the gods will provide. It has been getting so much worse these past few weeks that it seems now as if my stomach were as empty as a rich man`s brain. Why, even the rats have deserted our cottage, and there`s nothing left for poor Tabby, while old Blackfoot is nearly dead from starvation".

When the old woman referred to the sorrows of her pets, her remarks were answered by a pitiful mewing and woebegone barking from the corner where the two unfed creatures   were curled up together trying to keep warm.

Just then there was loud knocking at the gate. When the widow Wang called out, "Come in!" she was surprised to see an old-headed priest standing in the doorway. "Sorry, but we have nothing", she went on, feeling sure the visitor had come in search of food". We have fed on scraps these two weeks – on scraps and scrapings- and now we are living on the memories of what we used to have when my son`s father was living. Our cat was so fat she couldn`t climb to the roof. Now look at her. You can hardly see her, she`s so thin. No, I`m sorry we can`t help you, friend priest, but you see how it is".

"I didn`t come for alms", cried to the clean-shaven one, looking at her kindly, "but only to see what I could do to help you. The gods have listened long to the prayers of your devoted son. They honor him because he has not waited till you die to do sacrifice for you. They have seen how faithfully he has served you ever since his illness, and now, when he is worn out and unable to work, they are resolved to reward him for his virtue. You likewise have been a good mother and shall receive the gift I am now bringing".

"What do you mean?" faltered Mrs. Wang, hardly believing her ears at hearing a priest speak of bestowing mercies. "Have you come here to lough at our misfortunes?"

"By no means. Here in my hand I hold in tiny golden beetle which you will find has a magic power greater than any you ever dreamed of. I will leave this precious thing with you, a present from the god of filial conduct".

"Yes, it will sell for a good sum", murmured the other, looking closely at the trinket", and will give us millet for several days. Thanks, good priest, for your kindness".

"But you must by no means sell this golden beetle, for it has the power to fill your stomachs as long as you live".

The widow stared in open- mouthed wonder at the priest`s surprising words.

"Yes, you must not doubt me, but listen carefully to what I tell you. Whenever you wish food, you have only to place this ornament in a kettle of boiling water, saying over and over again the names of what you want to eat. In three minutes take off the lid, and there will be your dinner, smoking hot, and cooked more perfectly than any food you have ever eaten".

"May I try it now?", she asked eagerly.

"As soon as I am gone".

When the door was shut, the old woman hurriedly kindled of fire, boiled some water, and then dropped in the golden beetle, repeating these words again and again:

"Dumplings, dumplings, come to me,

I am thin as thin can be.

Dumplings, dumplings, smoking hot,

Dumplings, dumplings , fill the pot".

Would those three minutes never pass? Could the priest have told the truth?

Her old head was nearly wild with excitement as clouds of steam rose from the kettle. Off came the lid! She could wait no longer. Wonder of wonders! There before her unbelieving eyes was a pot, full to the brim of pork dumplings, dancing up and down in the bubbling water, the best, the most delicious dumplings she had ever tasted. She ate and ate till there was no room left in her greedy stomach, and then she feasted the cat and the dog until they were ready to burst.

"Good fortune has come at last", whispered Blackfoot, the dog, to Whitehead, the cat, as they lay down to sun themselves outside. "I fear I couldn`t have held out another week without running away to look for food. I don`t know just what`s happened, but there`s no use questioning the gods".

Mrs. Wang fairly danced for joy at the thought of her son`s return and of how she would feast him.

"Poor boy, how surprised he will be at our fortune – and it`s all on account of his goodness to his old mother".

When Ming-li came, with a dark cloud overhanging his brow, the widow saw plainly that disappointment was written there.

"Come, come, lad!", she cried cheerily, "clear up your face and smile, for the gods have been good to us and I shall soon show you how richly your devotion has been rewarded". So saying, she dropped the golden beetle into the boiling water and stirred up the fire.

Thinking his mother had gone stark mad for want of food, Ming-li stared solemnly at her. Anything was preferable to this misery. Should he sell his last outer garment for a few pennies and buy millet for her? Blackfoot licked his hand comfortingly, as if to say, "Cheer up, master, fortune has turned in our favour". Whitehead leaped upon a bench, purring like a sawmill.

Ming-li did not have long to wait. Almost in the twinkling of an eye he heard his mother crying out,

"Sit down at the table, son, and eat these dumplings while they are smoking hot".

Could he have heard correctly? Did his ears deceive him? No, there on the table was a huge platter full of the delicious pork dumplings he liked better than anything else in all the world, except, of course, his mother.

"Eat and ask no questions", counselled the Widow Wang. ``When you are satisfied I will tell you everything".

Wise advice! Very soon the young man`s chopsticks were twinkling like a little star in the verses. He ate long and happily, while his good mother watched him, her heart overflowing with joy at seeing him at last able to satisfy his hunger. But still the old woman could hardly wait for him to finish, she was so anxious to tell him her wonderful secret.

"Here, son!", she cried at last, as he began to pause between mouthfuls, "look at my treasure!" And she held out to him the golden beetle.

"First tell me what good fairy of a rich man has been filling our hands with silver?"

"That`s just what I am trying to tell you", she laughed, "for there was a fairy here this afternoon sure enough, only he was dressed like a bald priest. That golden beetle is all he gave me, but with it comes a secret worth thousands of cash to us".

The youth fingered the trinket idly, still doubting his senses, and waiting impatiently for the secret of his delicious dinner. "But, mother, what has this brass bauble to do with the dumplings, these wonderful pork dumplings, the finest I ever ate?"

"Baubles indeed! Brass! Fie, fie, my boy! You little know what you are saying. Only listen and you shall hear a tale that will open your eyes".

She then told him what had happened, and ended by setting all of the left-over dumplings upon the floor for Blackfoot and Whitehead, thing her son had never seen her do before, for they had been miserably poor and had had to save every scrap for the next meal.

Now began a long priod of perfect happiness. Mother, son, dog and cat -all enjoyed themselves to their hearts` content. All manner of new foods such as they had never tasted were called forth the pot by the wonderful little beetle. Bird- nest soup , shark`s fins, and a hundred other delicacies were theirs for the asking , and soon Ming-li regained all his strength , but, I fear, at the same time grew somewhat lazy, for it was no longer necessary for him to work. As for the two animals, they became fat and sleek and their hair grew long and glossy.

"HERE SON! SHE CRIED, "HAVE A LOOK AT MY TREASURE!"

But alas! According to Cinese proverb, pride invites sorrow. The little family became so proud of their good fortune that they began to ask friends and relatives to dinner that they might show off their good meals. One day a mr. and Mrs . Chu came from a distant village . They were much astonished at seeing the high style in which the Wangs lived. They had expected a beggar`s meal , but went away with full stomachs.

"It`s the best stuff I ever ate", said Mr. Chu, as they entered their own tumbledown house.

"Yes, and I know where it came from", exclaimed his wife. "I saw Widow Wang take a little gold ornament out of the pot and hide it in a cupboard. It must be some sort of charm, for I heard the mumbling to herself about pork and dumplings just as she was stirring up the fire".

"A charm, eh? Why is it that other people have all the luck? It looks as if we were doomed forever to be poor".

"Why not borrow Mrs. Wang`s charm for a few days until we can pick up a little flesh to keep our bones from clattering? Turn about`s fairy play. Of course, we`ll return it sooner or later".

"Doubtless they very close watch over it. When would you find them away from home, now that they don`t have to work anymore? As their house only contains one room, and that no bigger than ours, it would be difficult to borrow this golden trinket. It is harder , for more reasons than one, to steal from a beggar than from a king".

"Luck is surely with us", cried Mrs. Chu, clapping her hands. "They are going this very day to the Temple fair. I overhead Mrs. Wang tell her son that he must not forget he was to take her about the middle of the afternoon. I will slip back then and borrow the little vharm from the box in which she hid it".

"Aren`t you afraid of Balckfoot?"

"Pooh! He`s so fat he can do nothing but roll. If the widow comes back suddenly, I`ll tell her I came to look for my big hair- pin, that I lost it while I was at dinner".

"All right, go ahead, only of course we must remember we`re borrowing the thing, not stealing it, for the Wangs have always been good friends to us, and then, too, we have just dined with them".

So skillfully did this crafty woman carry out her plans that within an hour she was back in her own house, gleefully showing the priest`s charm to her husband. Not a soul had seen her enter the Wang house. The dog had made no noise, and the cat had only blinked her surprise at seeing a stranger and had gone to sleep again on the floor.

Great was the clamour and weeping when , on returning from the fair in expectation of a hot supper, the widow found her treasure missing. It was long before she could grasp the truth. She went back to the little box in the cupboard ten times before she could believe it was empty , and the room looked as if a cyclone had struck it, so long and carefully did the two unfortunates hunt for the lost beetle.

Then came days of hunger which were all the harder to bear since the recent period of good food and plenty. Oh, if they had only not got used to such dainties! How hard it was to go back to scraps and scrapings!

But if the widow and her son were sad over the loss of the good meals, the two pets were even more so. They were reduced to beggary and had to go froth daily upon the streets in search of stray bones and refuse that decent dogs and cats turned up their noses at.

One day after this period of starvation had been going on for some time, Whitehead began suddenly to frisk about in great excitement.

"Whatever is the matter with you?" growled Blackfoot. ``Are you mad from hunger, or have you caught another flea?"

"I was just thinking over our affairs, and now I know the cause of all our trouble".

"Do you indeed?" sneered Blackfoot.

"Yes, I do indeed, and you`d better think twice before you mock me, for I hold your future in my paw, as you will very soon see".

"Well, you needn`t get angry about nothing. What wonderful discovery have you made- That every rat has one tail?"

"First of all, are you willing to help me bring good fortune back to our family?"

"of course I am. Don`t be silly, "barked the dog, wagging his tail joyfully at the thought of another good dinner. "Surely! Surely! I will do anything you like if it will bring Dame fortune back again".

"All right. Here is the plan. There has been a thief in the house who has stolen our mistress`s golden beetle. You remember all our big dinners that came from the pot? Well, every day I saw our mistress take a little golden beetle out of the black box and put it into the pot. One day she held it up before me, saying, "Look, puss, there is the cause of all our happiness. Don`t you wish it was yours?" Then she laughed and put it back into the box that stays in the cupboard".

"Is that true?" questioned Blackfoot. "Why didn`t you say something about it before?"

"You remember the day Mr. and Mrs. Chu were here, and how Mrs. Chu returned in the afternoon after master and mistress had gone to the fair? I saw her, out of the tail of my eye, go to that very black box and take out the golden beetle. I thought it curious, but never dreamed she was a thief. Alas! I was wrong! She took the beetle, and if I am notmistaken, she and her husband are now enjoying the feasts that belong to us".

"Let`s claw them", growled black foot, gnashing his teeth.

"That would do no good", counselled the other, "for they would be sure to come out best in the end. We want the beetle back- that`s the main thing. We`ll leave revenge to human beings; it is none of our business".

"What do you suggest?" said Blackfoot. "I am with you through thick and thin".

"Let`s go to the chu house and make off with the beetle".

"Alas, that I am not a cat!" moaned Blackfoot. "If we go there I couldn`t get inside, for robbers always keep their gates well locked. If I were like you I could scale the wall. It is the first time in all my life I ever envied a cat".

"We will go together", continued Whitehead. "I will ride on your back when we are fording the river, and you can protect me from strange animals. When we get to the Chu house, I will climb over the wall and manage the rest of the business myself. Only you must wait outside to help me to get home with the prize".

No sooner arranged than done. The companions set out that very night on their adventure. They crossed the river as the cat had suggested, and Blackfoot really enjoyed the swim, for, as he said, it took him back to his puppyhood, while they reached the Chu house.

"Just wait till I return", purred Whitehead in Blackfoot`s eye.

With a mighty spring she reached the top of the mud wall, and then jumped down to the inside court. While she was resting in the shadow, trying to decide just how to go about her work, a slight rustling attracted her attention, and pop! One giant spring, one stretch- out of the claws, and she had caught a rat that had just come out of his hole for a drink and a midnight walk.

Now, whitehead was so hungry that she would have made short work of this tempting prey if the rat had not opened its mouth and, to her amazement, begun to talk in good cat dialect.

"Pray, good puss, not so fast with your sharp teeth! Kindly be careful with your claws! Don`t you know it is the custom now to put prisoners on their honor? I will promise not to turn away"

"Poor! What honor has a rat?"

"Much good it would do you", purred Whitehead, her fur crackling noisily, and her mouth watering for a taste of rat steak. "However, I am quite willing to put you to the test. First, answer a few polite questions and I will see if you`re a truthful fellow. What kind of food is your master eating now, that you should be round and plump when I am thin and scrawny?"

"Oh, we have been in luck lately, I can tell you. Master and mistress feed on the fat of the land, and of course we hangers-on get the crumbs".

"But this is a por tumble- down house. How can they afford such eating?"

"That is great secret, but as I am in honor bound to tell you, here goes. My mistress has just obtained I some manner or other, a fairy`s charm...".

"She stole it from our place, "hissed the cat, "I will claw her eyes out if I get the chance. Why, we`ve been fairly starving for want of that beetle. She stole it from us just after she had been an invited guest! What do you think of that for honor, Sir Rat? Were your mistress`s ancestors' followers of the sage?"

"Oh, oh, oh! Why, that explains everything!", wailed the rat. "I have often wondered how they got the golden beetle, and yet of course I dared not ask any questions".

"No, certainly not! But hark you, friend rat you get that golden trinket back for me, and I will set you free at once obligations. Do you know where she hides it?"

"Yes, in a crevice where the wall is broken. I will bring it to you in jiffy, but how shall we exist when our charm is gone? There will be a season of scanty food, I fear; beggars` fare for all of us".

"Live on the memory of your good deed", purred the cat. "It is splendid, you know, to be an honest beggar. Now scoot! I trust you completely, since your people lived in the home of Confucius. I will wait here for your return. Ah!", laughed Whitehead to herself, "luck seems to be coming our way again!"

Five minutes later the rat appeared, bearing the trinket in its mouth. It passed the beetle over to the cat, and then with a whisk was off forever. Its honor was safe, but it was afraid of Whitehead. It had seen the gleam of desire in her green eyes, and the cat might have broken her word if she had not she had not been so anxious to get back home where her mistress could command the wonderful kettle once more to bring forth food.

The two adventurers reached the river just as the sun was rising above the eastern hills.

"Be careful", cautioned Blackfoot, as the cat leaped upon his back for ride across the stream, "be careful not to forget the treasure. In short, remember that even though you are a female, it is necessary to keep your mouth closed till we reach the other side".

"Thanks, but I don`t think I need your advice", replied Whitehead, picking up the beetle and leaping on to the dog`s back.

But alas! Just as they were nearing the farther shore, the excited cat forgot her wisdom for a moment. A fish suddenly leaped out of the water directly under her nose. It was too great a temptation. Snap! Went her jaws in a vain effort to land the scaly treasure, and the golden beetle sank to the bottom of the river.

"There!" said the dog angrily, "what did I tell you? Now all trouble has been in vain- all on account of your stupidity".

For a little time, there was a bitter dispute, and the companions called each other some very bad names- such as turtle and rabbit. Just as they were starting away from the river, disappointed and discouraged, a friendly frog who had by chance heard their conversation offered to fetch the treasure from the bottom of the stream. No sooner said than done, and after thanking this accommodating animal profusely, they turned homeward once more.

When they reached the cottage the door was shut, and, bark as he would, Blackfoot could not persuade his master to open it. There was the sound of loud wailing inside.

"Mistress is broken- hearted whispered the cat, "I will go to her and make her happy".

So saying, she sprang lightly through a hole in the paper window, which, alas! Was too small and too far from the ground for the faithful dog to enter.

A sad sight greeted the gaze of Whitehead. The son was lying on the bed unconscious, almost dead for want of food, while his mother, in despair, was rocking backwards and forwards wringing her wrinkled hands and crying at the top of her voice for some one to come and save them.

"Here I am, mistress", cried Whitehead, "and here is the treasure you are weeping for. I have rescued it and brought it back to you".

The widow, wild with joy at sight of the beetle, seized the cat in her scrawny arms and hugged the pet tightly to her bosom.

"Breakfast, son, breakfast! Wake up from your swoon! Fortune has come again. We are saved from starvation!"

Soon a steaming hot meal was ready, and you may well imagine how the old woman and her son, heaping praises upon Whitehead, filled the beast`s platter with good things, but never a word did they say of the faithful dog, who remained outside sniffing the fragrant odors and waiting in sad wonder, for all this time the artful cat had said nothing of Blackfoot`s part in the rescue of the golden beetle.

At last, when breakfast was over, slipping away from the others, Whitehead jumped out through the hole in the window.

"Oh, my dear Blackfoot", she began laughingly, "you should have been inside to see what a feast they gave me! Mistress was so delighted at my bringing back her treasure that she could not give me enough to eat, nor say enough kind things about me. Too bad, old fellow, that you are hungry. You`d better run out into the street and hunt up a bone".

Maddened by the shameful treachery of his companion, the enraged dog sprang upon the cat and in a few seconds had shaken her to death.

"So dies the one who forgets a friend who loses honor", he cried sadly, as he stood over the body of his companion.

Rushing out into the street, he proclaimed the treachery of Whitehead to the members of his tribe, at the same time advising that all self-respecting dogs should from that time onwards make war upon the feline race.

And that is why the descendants of old Blackfoot, whether in China or in the great countries of the West, have waged continual war upon the children and grandchildren of Whitehead, for a thousand generations of dogs have fought them and hated them with a great and lasting hatred.

(HANS ANDERSEN`S FAIRY TALES)

VOCABULARY

Slight – yengil

Widow – beva ayol

Coppers – chaqa

Cheerfully – shod

Extreme cold – qattiq sovuq

Deep snow – qalin qor

Violent winds- kuchli shamol

To suffer – azoblanmoq

To fall – qulamoq

To weigh down- og`irlik qilmoq

A hurricane – dovul, bo`ron

Blown – esmoq

Scant – kam, qizg`anmoq

Medicine – dori

Arose – turmoq, paydo bo`lmoq

Sickbed – to`shak

Sorrow – g`am

A cottage – hovli, dala uy

Starvation – ochlik

A pitiful – achinarli

An old- headed – qari

Priest – ruhoniy

Doorway – kiraverish, ostona

Sacrifice – qurbon qilmoq, voz kechmoq

Likewise – shu tarzda

Millet – tariq

Trinket – mayda- chuyda bezak

Steam – bug`

Overhanging – o`simtalar

Stark – butunlay

Solemnly – tantanali ravishda

Twinkling – charaqlamoq

Sleek – silliq

Charm – joziba, maftun etmoq

Dainties – shirinlik

Stupidity – ahmoqlik

Shameful - uyatli

CATS DON`T CARE

Cats don`t care what dogs think

They just look down any sort a wink.

Perch themselves, way up high

The dogs bark and start to cry.

It`s really not fair, those all cats

Hiding in places, just like rats.

The dogs want to play, join in the fun

 Chase that cat, make it run.

But cats care less, don`t need to play fair

Like to tease, don`t have a care.

Poor dogs sit and wonder why?

Sly old cat naps with a sigh

Dogs keep guard, waiting for a twitch

Cat doesn`t move, not even for an itch.

The game goes on, cat unaware

 The dogs just plead, please care

PROVERBS

A grateful dog has more worth than an ungrateful man

(Minnatdor itning noshukur odamdan ko`proq qiymati bor)

A white dog does not bite another white dog

(Oq it oq itni tishlamas)

The barking of a dog does not disturb the man on a camel

(Itning hurishi tuyadagi odamni bezovta qilmaydi)

The dogs bark, but the caravan moves on

(It hurar karvon o`tar)

An old cat likes young mice

(Qari mushuk yosh sichqonlarni yoqtirar)

Two cats will not live together in one sack

(Bir xaltada ikkita mushuk yashamas)

Cats don`t catch the old birds

(Mushuklar qari qushlarni ovlamaydi)

A cat in a cage becomes a lion

(Qafasdagi mushuk ilonga aylanar)

THE TALKING FISH

(CHINESE FOLKTALE)

Long, long before your great-grandfather was born there lived in the village of Everlasting Happiness two men called Li and Sing. Now, these two men were close friends, living together in the same house. Before settling down in the village of Everlasting Happiness they had ruled as high officials for more than twenty years. They had often treated the people very harshly, so that everybody, old and young, disliked and hated them. And yet, by robbing the wealthy merchants and by cheating the poor, these two evil companions had become rich, and it was in order to spend their ill-gotten gains in idle amusements that they sought out the village of Everlasting Happiness. "For here", said they, ``we can surely find that joy which has been denied us in every other place. Here we shall no longer be scorned by men and reviled by women".

Consequently, these two men bought for themselves the finest house in the village, furnished it in the most elegant manner, and decorated the walls with scrolls filled with wise sayings and pictures by famous artists. Outside there were lovely gardens filled with flowers and birds, and oh, ever so many trees with queer twisted branches growing in the shape of tigers and other wild animals.

Whenever they felt lonely Li and Sing invited rich people of the neighborhood to come and dine with them, and after they had eaten, sometimes they would go out upon the little lake in the center of their estate, rowing in an awkward flat-bottomed boat that had been built by the village carpenter.

One day, on such an occasion, when the sun had been beating down fiercely upon the clean-shaven heads of all those on the little barge, for you must know this was long before the day when hats were worn—at least, in the village of Everlasting Happiness—Mr. Li was suddenly seized with a giddy feeling, which rapidly grew worse and worse until he was in a burning fever.

"Snake`s blood mixed with powdered deer-horn is the thing for him", said the wise-looking doctor who was called in, peering at li carefully through his huge glasses, "Be sure", he continued, addressing Li`s personal attendant, and, at the same time, snapping his long finger-nails nervously, "be sure, above all, not to leave him alone, for he is in danger of going raving mad at any moment , and I cannot say what he may do if he is not looked after carefully. A man in his condition has no more sense than a baby".

Now, although these words of the doctor`s really made Mr. Li angry, he was too ill to reply, for all this time his head had been growing hotter and hotter, until at last a feverish sleep overtook him. No sooner had he closed his eyes than his faithful servant, half-famished, rushed out of the room to join his fellows at their midday meal.

Li awoke with a start, he had slept only ten minutes. "Water, water", he moaned, "bathe my head with cold water. I am half dead with pain!" But there was no reply, for the attendant was dining happily with his fellows.

"Air, air", groaned Mr. Li, tugging at the collar of his silk shirt. "I`m dying for water. I`m starving for air. This blazing heat will kill me. It is hotter than the Fire god himself ever dreamed of making it. Wang, wang!" clapping his hands febbly and calling to his servant", air and water , air and water!"

But still no Wang.

At last, with the strength that is said to come from despair, Mr. Li arose from his couch and staggered toward the doorway. Out he went the paved courtyard, and then, after only a moment`s hesitation, made his way across it into narrow passage that led into the lake garden.

"What do they care for a man when he is sick?" he muttered. "My good friend Sing is doubtless even now enjoying his afternoon nap, with a servant standing by to fan him, and a block of ice near his head to cool the air. What does he care if I die of a raging fever? Doubtless he expects to inherit all my money. And my servants! That rascal Wang has been with me these ten years, living on me and growing lazier every season! What does he care if I pass away? Doubtless he is certain that sing`s servants will think of something for him to do, and he will have even less work than he has now. Water, water! I shall die if I don`t soon find a place to soak myself!"

So saying, he arrived at the bank of a little brook that flowed in through a water gate at one side of the garden and emptied itself into the big fish-pond. Flinging himself down by a little stream Li bathed his hands and wrists in the cool water. How delightful! If only it were deep enough to cover his whole body, how gladly would he cast himself in and enjoy the bliss of its refreshing embrace!

For a long time, he lay on the ground, rejoicing at his escape from the doctor`s clutches. Then, as the fever began to rise again, he sprang up with a determined cry, "What am I waiting for? I will do it. There`s no one to prevent me, and it will do me a world of good. I will cast myself head first into the fish-pond. It is not deep enough near the shore to drown me if I should be too weak to swim, and I am sure it will restore me to strength and health".

He hastened along the little stream, almost running in his eagerness to reach the deeper water of the pond. He was like some small Tom Brown who had escaped from the watchful eye of the master and run out to play in a forbidden spot.

Hark! Was that a servant calling? Had Wang discovered the absence of his employer? Would he sound the alarm, and would the whole place soon be alive with men searching for the fever-stricken patient?

With one last sigh of satisfaction Li flung himself, clothes and all, into the quiet waters of the fish-pond. Now Li had been brought up in Fukien province on the seashore, and was a skillful swimmer. He dived and splashed to his heart`s content, then floated on the surface. "It takes me back to my boyhood", he cried, ``why, oh why, is it not the fashion to swim? I`d love to live in the water all the time and yet some of my countrymen are even more afraid than a cat of getting their feet wet. As for me, I`d give anything to stay here forever".

"You would, eh?" chuckled a hoarse voice just under him, and then there was a sort of wheezing sound, followed by a loud burst of laughter. Mr. Li jumped as if an arrow had struck him, but when he noticed the fat, ugly monster below, his fear turned into anger. ``Look here, what do you mean by giving a fellow such a start! Don`t you know what the Classics say about such rudeness?"

The giant fish laughed all the louder. "What time do you suppose I have for Classics? You make me laugh till I cry!"

"But you must answer my question", cried Mr. Li, more and more persistently, forgetting for the moment that he was not trying some poor culprit for a petty crime. "Why did you laugh? Speak out at once, fellow!"

"Well, since you are such a saucy piece". roared the other, "I will tell you. It was because you awkward creatures, who call yourselves men, the most highly civilized beings in the world, always think you understand a thing fully when you have only just found out how to do it".

"You are talking about the island dwarfs, the Japanese", interrupted Mr. Li, ``We Chinese seldom undertake to do anything new".

"Just hear the man!" chuckled the fish. "Now, fancy your wishing to stay in the water forever! What do you know about water? Why you`re not even provided with the proper equipment for swimming. What would you do if you really lived here always?"

"What am I doing now?" spluttered Mr. Li, so angry that he sucked in a mouthful of water before he knew it.

"Floundering", retorted the other.

"Don`t you see me swimming? Are those big eyes of yours made of glass?"

"Yes, I see you all right", guffawed the fish, "that's just it! I see you too well. Why you tumble about as awkwardly as a water buffalo wallowing in a mud puddle!"

Now, as Mr. Li had always considered himself an expert in water sports, he was, by the time, speechless with rage, and all he could do was to paddle feebly round and round with strokes just strong enough to keep himself from sinking.

"Then, too", continued the fish, more and more calm as the other lost his temper, "you have a very poor arrangement for breathing. If I am not mistaken, at the bottom of this pond you would find yourself worse off than I should be at the top of a palm tree. What would you do to keep yourself from starving? Do you think it would be convenient if you had to flop yourself out on to the land every time you wanted a bite to eat? And yet, being a man, I doubt seriously if you would be content to take the proper food for fishes. You have hardly a single feature that would make you contented if you were to join an under-water school. Look at your clothes, too, water-soaked and heavy. Do you think them suitable to protect you from cold and sickness? Nature forgot to give you any scales. Now I'm going to tell you a joke, so you must be sure to laugh. Fishes are like grocery shops— always judged by their scales. As you haven't a sign of a scale, how will people judge you? See the point, eh? Nature gave you a skin, but forgot the outer covering, except, perhaps at the ends of your fingers and your toes you surely see by this time why I consider your idea ridiculous?"

Sure enough, in spite of his recent severe attack of fever, Mr. Li had really cooled completely off. He had never understood before what great disadvantages there were connected with being a man. Why not make use of this acquaintance, find out from him how to get rid of that miserable possession he had called his manhood, and gain the delights that only a fish can have? "Then, are you indeed contented with your lot?", he asked finally. Are there not moments when you would prefer to be a man?"

"I, a man!" thundered the other, lashing the water with his tail. "How dare you suggest such a disgraceful change! Can it be that you do not know my rank? Why my fellow, you behold in me a favorite nephew of the king!"

"Then, may it please your lordship", said Mr. Li, softly, "I should be exceedingly grateful if you would speak a kind word for me to your master into a fish and accept me as a subject?"

"Of course!" replied the other, "all things are possible to the king. Know you not that my sovereign is a loyal descendant of the great water dragon, and, as such, can never die, but lives on and on and on, forever, and ever, and ever, like the ruling house of Japan?"

"Oh, oh!" gasped Mr. Li, "even the Son of Heaven , our most worshipful emperor, cannot boast of such long years. Yes, I would give my fortune to be a follower of your imperial master".

"Then follow me", laughed the other, starting off at a rate that made the water hiss and boil for ten feet around him.

Mr. Li struggled vainly to keep up. If he had thought himself a good swimmer, he now saw his mistake and every bit of remaining pride was torn to tatters. "Please wait a moment", he cried out politely, "I beg of you to remember that I am only a man!"

"Pardon me", replied the other, "It was stupid of me to forget, especially as I had just been talking about it".

Soon they reached a sheltered inlet at the farther side of the pond. There Mr. Li saw a gigantic carp idly floating about in shallow pool, and then lazily flirting his huge tail of fluttering his fins proudly from side to side. Attendant courtiers darted hither and thither, ready to do the master`s slightest bidding. One of them, splendidly attired in royal scarlet, announced, with a downward flip of the head, the approach of the King`s nephew who was leading Mr. Li to an audience with his Majesty.

"Whom have you here, my lad?", began the ruler, as his nephew, hesitating for words to explain his strange request, moved his fins nervously backwards and forwards. "Strange company, it seems to me, you are keeping these days".

"Only a poor man, most royal sir", replied the other, "who beseeches your Highness to grant him your gracious favor".

"When man asks favor of a fish,

``Tis hard to penetrate his wish—

He often seeks a lordly dish

To serve upon his table".

Repeated the king, smiling. ``And yet, nephew, you think this fellow is really peaceably inclined and is not coming among us as a spy?"

Before his friend could answer, Mr. Li had cast himself upon his knees in the shallow water, before the noble carp, and bowed thrice, until his face was daubed with mud from the bottom of the pool. ``Indeed, your Majesty, I am only a poor mortal who seeks your kindly grace. If you would but consent to receive me into your school of fishes. I would forever be your ardent admirer and your lowly slave".

"In sooth, the fellow talks as if in earnest", remarked the king,   after a moment`s reflection", and though the request is, perhaps, the strangest to which I have ever listened, I really see no reason why I should not turn a fish year. But, have the goodness first to cease your bowing. You are stirring up enough mud to plaster the royal place of a shark".

Poor Li, blushing at the monarch`s reproof, waited patiently for the answer to his request.

"Very well, so be it", cried the king impulsively, "your wish is granted. Sir Trout", turning to one of his courtiers, "bring hither a fish-skin of proper size for this ambitious fellow".

No sooner said than done. The fish skin was slipped over Mr. Li`s head, and his whole body was soon tucked snugly away in the scaly coat. Only his arms remained uncovered. In the twinkling of an eye Li felt sharp pains shoot through every part of his body. His arms began to shrivel up and his hands changed little by little until they made an excellent pair of fins, just as good as those of the king himself. As for his legs and feet, they suddenly began to stick together until , wriggle as he would, Li could not separate them . "Ah, ha!" thought he, "my kicking days are over, for my toes are now turned into a first-class tail".

"Not so fast". laughed the king, as Li, after thanking the royal personage profusely, started out to try his new fins; "not so fast, my friend. Before you depart, perhaps I`d better give you a little friendly advice, else your new powers are likely to land you on the hook of some lucky fisherman, and you will find yourself served up as a prize of the pond".

"I will gladly listen to your lordly counsel, for the words of the Most High to his lovely slave are like pearls before sea slugs. However, as I was once a man myself I think I understand the simple tricks they use to catch us fish, and I am therefore in position to avoid trouble".

"Don`t be so sure about it. "A hungry carp of ten falls into danger", as one of our sages so wisely remarked. There are two cautions I would impress upon you. One is, never, never, eat a dangling worm; no matter how tempting it looks there sure to be horrible hooks inside. Secondly, always swim like lighting if you see a net, nut in the opposite direction. Now, I will have you served your first meal out of the royal pantry, but after that, you must hunt for yourself, like every other self-respecting citizen of the watery world".

After Li had been fed with several slugs, followed by a juicy worm of dessert, and after again thanking the king and the king`s nephew for their kindness, he started forth to test his tail and fins. It was no easy matter, at first, to move them properly. A single flirt of the tail, no more vigorous than those he had been used to giving with his legs, would send him whirling round and round in the water, for all the world like a living top; and when he wriggled his fins, ever so slightly, as he thought, he found himself sprawling on his back in a most ridiculous fashion for a dignified member of fish kind. It took several hours of constant practice to get the proper stroke, and then he found he could move about without being conscious of any effort. It was the easiest thing he had ever done in his life; and oh! The water was so cool and delightful! ``Would that I might enjoy that endless life the poets write off!", he murmured blissfully.

Many hours passed by until at last Li was compelled to admit that, although he was not tired, he was certainly hungry. How to get something to eat? Oh! Why had he not asked the friendly nephew a few simple questions? How easily his lordship might have told him the way to get a good breakfast! But alas! Without such advice, it would be a whale`s task to accomplish it. Hither and thither the swam, into the deep still water, and along the muddy shore; down, down to the pebbly bottom—always looking, looking for a tempting worm. He dived into the weeds and rushes, poked his nose among the lily pads. All for nothing! No fly or worm of any kind to gladden his eager eyes! Another hour passed slowly away, and all the time his hunger was growing greater and greater. Would the fish god, the mighty dragon, not grant him even one little morsel to satisfy his aching stomach, especially since, now that he was a fish, he had no way of tightening up his belt, as hungry soldiers do when they are on a forced march?

Just as Li was beginning to think he could not wriggle his tail an instant longer, and that soon, very soon, he would feel himself slipping, slipping, slipping down to the bottom of the pond to die—at that very moment, chancing to look up, he saw, oh joy! A delicious red worm dangling a few inches above his nose. The sight gave new strength to his weary fins and tail. Another minute, and he would have had the delicate morsel in his mouth, when alas! He chanced to recall the advice given him the day before by great King Carp. "No matter how tempting it looks, there sure to be horrible hooks inside". For an instant Li hesitated. The worm floated a trifle nearer to his half-open mouth. How tempting! After all, what was a hook to a fish when he was dying? Why be a coward? Perhaps this worm was an exception to the rule, or perhaps, perhaps, ant thing-really a fish in such a plight as Mr. Li could not be expected to follow advice-even the advice of a real King.

Pop! He had it in his mouth. Oh, soft morsel, worthy of a king`s desire! Now he could laugh at words of wisdom, and eat whatever came before his eye. But ugh! What was that strange feeling that-Ouch! It was the fatal hook!

With one frantic jerk, and a hundred twists and turns, poor Li sought to pull away from the cruel burb that stuck so fast in the roof of his mouth. It was now too late to wish he had kept away from temptation. Better far to have starved at the bottom of the cool pond than to be jerked out by some miserable fisherman to the light and sunshine of the busy world. Nearer and nearer he approached the surface. The more he struggled the sharper grew the cruel barb. Then, with one final splash, he found himself dangling in mid-air, swinging helplessly at the end of a long line. With a chunk he fell into a flat-bottomed boat, directly on top of several smaller fish.

"Ah, a carp!", shouted a well-known voice gleefully; ``the biggest fish I have caught these three moons. What good luck!"

It was the voice of old Chang, the fisherman, who had been supplying Mr. Li`s table ever since that official`s arrival in the village of Everlasting Happiness. Only a word of a explanation, and he, Li, would be free once more to swim about where he willed. And Then there should be no more barbs for him. An escaped fish fears the hook.

"I say, Chang", he began, gasping for breath, "really now, you must chuck me overboard at once, for, don`t you see, I am Mr. Li, your old master. Come, hurry up about it. I`ll excuse you this time for your mistake, for, of course, you had no way of knowing. Quick!"

But Chang, with a savage jerk, pulled the hook from Li`s mouth, and looked idly towards the pile of glistening fish, gloating over his catch, and wondering how much money he could demand for it. He had heard nothing of Mr. Li`s remarks, for Chang had been deaf since childhood.

"Quick, quick, I am dying for air moaned poor Li, and then, with a groan, he remembered the fisherman`s affliction.

By this time, they had arrived at the shore, and Li, in company with his fellow victims, found himself suddenly thrown into a whicker basket. Oh, the horrors of that journey on land! Only a tiny bit of water remained in the closely-woven thing. It was all he could do the breath.

Joy of joys! At the door of his own house he saw his good friend Sing just coming out. "Hey, sing", he shouted, at the top of his voice, ``help, help! This son of a turtle wants to murder me. He has me in here with these fish, and doesn`t seem to know that I am Li, his master. Kindly order him to take me to the lake and throw me in, for it`s cool there and I like the water life much better than that on land".

Li paused to hear Sing`s reply, but there came not a single word.

"I beg your honor to have a look at my catch", said old Chang to Sing. "Here is the finest fish of the season. I have brought him here so that you and my honoured master, Mr. Li, may have a treat. Carp is his favorite delicacy".

"Very kind of you, my good Chang, I`m sure, but I fear poor Mr. Li will not eat fish for some time. He has a bad attack of fever".

"There is where you`re wrong", shouted Li, from his basket, flopping about with all his might, to attract attention, "I`m going to die of a chill. Can`t you recognize your old friend? Help me out of this trouble and you may have all my money for your pains".

"Hey, what`s that!", questioned Sing, attracted, as usual, by the word money. "Shades of Confucius! It sounds as if the carp were talking".

"What, a talking fish", laughed Chang. "Why, master, I`ve lined nigh on to sixty years, and such a fish has never come under my sight. There are talking birds and talking beasts for that matter; but talking fish, who ever heard of such a wonder? No, I think your ears must have deceived you, but this carp will surely cause talk when I get him into the kitchen. I`m sure the cook has ever seen his like. Oh, master! I hope you will be hungry when you sit down to this fish. What a pity Mr. Li couldn`t help you to devour it!".

"Help to devour myself, eh?" grumbled poor Li, now almost dead for lack of water. "You must take me for a cannibal, or some other sort of savage".

Old Chang had now gone round the house to the servant`s quarters, and, after calling out the cook, held up poor Li by the tail for the chef to inspect.

With a mighty jerk Li tore himself away and fell at the feet of his faithful cook. "Save me, save me!", he cried out in despair", this measurable Chang is deaf and doesn`t know that I am Mr. Li, his master. My fish voice is not string enough for his hearing. Only take me back to the pond and set me free. You shall have a pension for life, wear good clothes and eat good food, all the rest of your days. Only hear me and obey! Listen, my dear cook, listen!"

``The thing seems to be talking", muttered the cook, ``but such wonders cannot be. Only ignorant old women or foreigners would believe that a fish could talk". And seizing his former master by the tail, he swung him on to a table, picked up a knife, and began to whet it on a stone.

"Oh, oh!", screamed Li, "you will stick a knife into me! You will scrape off my beautiful shiny scales! You will whack off my lovely new fins! You will murder your old master!"

"Well you won`t talk much longer", growled the cook, ``I`ll show you a trick or two with the blade".

So saying, with gigantic thrust, he plunged the knife deep into the body of the trembling victim.

With a shrill cry of horror and despair, Mr. Li awoke from the deep into which he ha fallen. His fever was gone, but he found himself trembling with fear at thought of the terrible death that had come to him in dreamland.

"Thanks be to Buddha, I am not a fish!" he cried out joyfully, and now I shall be well enough to enjoy the feast to which Mr. Sing has bidden guests for tomorrow. But alas, now that I can eat the old fisherman`s prize carp, it has changed back into myself.

"If only the good of our dreams come true,

I shouldn`t mind dreaming the whole day through".

(HANS ANDERSEN`S FAIRY TALES)

VOCABULARY

Settle down – joylashmoq

Companion – hamroh

Consequently – natijada

Queer – g`alatiroq

Whenever – qachonki

Awkward – qo`pol

Flat- bottom – tekis- pastki

Suddenly – kutilmaganda

Giddy – boshni aylantiruvchi

Fellow – o`rtoq

Awoke – uyg`otmoq

Strength – qattiqlik

Pass away – vafot etmoq

Boyhood – o`smirlik

Arrow – nayza

Floundering - intilayotgan

THE LITTLE FISH

One little fish

Swam in his dish

He blew bubbles

And made a wish.

All he wanted

Was another fish

To swim with him

In his little dish

Another fish

Came one day

To blow bubbles

While they played

Two little fish

Blowing bubbles

In the dish

Swimming around

Singing plish, plish, plish.

PROVERBS

Big fish eat little fish

(Katta baliq kichik baliqni yeydi)

Who owns the bank, owns the fish.

(Kim bankni egallasa, baliqni egallagan bo`ladi)

Nothing is so clean as a fish

(Hech narsa baliqchalik pok emas)

All rotten fish taste the same

(Barcha chirigan baliqning ta`mi bir)

There is no need for fish in the empty pond

(Bo`sh hovuzda baliqqa ehtiyoj yo`q)

To lie and eat fish demand a lot of skill

(Yolg`on gapirish va baliq yeyish katta mahurat talab qiladi)

THE CLEVER WIFE

Long ago, there lived a lazy man. He never wanted to work, and was always looking for an easy way to get food. One day, as he was passing by a temple, he saw a mango tree full of juicy mangoes. He climbed up on the compound wall of the temple to steal the mangoes.

 The temple also had a pond full of fish. As soon as the lazy man noticed the fish, he jumped into the compound. Being lazy, he didn`t even bother to bend. He used his hands to pluck the mangoes and his feet to catch the fish. Stuffing both in his bag, he ran home. "Here, I have brought some good food today", he said to his wife, taking out the fish and some mangoes from his bag.

At first, his wife excited to see such delicious food as they had not eaten mangoes and fish for a long time. But then she thought, "he never goes to work; how did he manage to bring home the mangoes and the fish?" She took the bag from her husband and asked", Where did you get these from, dear?" The husband said with pride", I stole them from the temple compound". The wife was shocked to hear this!" Earlier my husband was lazy, now he has become a thief too! How shameful!" she thought.

So, the clever wife decided to teach her lazy husband a lesson. She pretended to be happy and said", Good that you stole from the temple compound; there are plenty of mangoes and fish there. I will prepare a delicious feast today. Go and take a bath in the meantime",

With happy thoughts of the feast, the man went to take a bath which his wife went into kitchen to cook the fish. As she prepared the meal, its mouth-watering aroma spread in the entire house. "Hair can`t resist the temptation!" thought the lazy man, finishing his bath, quickly. His mouth began to water. ``Come quickly, dear!" called out his wife. "The food is almost ready".

Just as she heard her husband`s footsteps, she quickly untied her hair, picked up the pan of fish in her hand and stood up.

 As soon as her husband entered the kitchen, he saw a horrid- looking figure staring at him. ``How dare you steal from my temple?" yelled the wife. "W…What! Your temple!" asked the man, scared. "Yes, I am the Goddess of the temple", replied the wife angrily. "I saw you stealing from my mango tree and my pond! Now I have taken possession of your wife`s body. And I am going to kill you!" Hearing this, the man fell to his knees and begged for mercy". Then go and throw this vessel of fish into the pond and swear by me that you won`t be lazy anymore, and that you will work hard, and that you will never steal again", said the wife. "I promise, O Goddess!" said the man.

He threw the vessel of fish in the pond and vowed never steal again. From that day on, he was a changed man and not lazy anymore. Thus, the clever wife had taught her husband a valuable lesson.

VOCABULARY

Temple – ibodatxona

A mango tree – mango daraxti

Climb up – yuqoriga chiqmoq

To steal – o`g`irlamoq

A pond – hovuz

To bring- keltirmoq

To stuff – to`ldirmoq

A husband – er, turmush o`rtoq

To pretend – mug`ambirlik qilmoq

Delicious – mazzali

Feast – ziyofat

Shameful – uyatli

Meantime – bu orada

Scared – qo`rqqan

Anymore – boshqa umuman emas

GOOD HABITS & BAD HABITS

We are the slaves of our habits,

It makes our character

It defines our destiny

Our thoughts are the seeds of it,

Our action its initiation.

Bad habits degrade us

Leads us towards doom

While we may not be aware

But will face the ultimate reality soon.

Good habits bring richness

Richness in mind, body and soul

It requires effort to inculcate but leads us towards our goal.

We cannot escape,

Will have to choose between the two.

To be the slave of good habits,

We will have to be the master of our thoughts.

PROVERBS

Old habits die hard

(Eski odatlarning o`lishi qiyin)

A good name is better than good habits

(Yaxshi nom, yaxshi odatdan afzal)

Habit is a shirt that we wear till death

(Odat- bu biz o`limgacha kiyadigan ko`ylak)

Good habits result from resisting temptation

(Yaxshi odatlar vasvasaga qarshi turishdan kelib chiqadi)

Wasting is a bad habit,

Saving is a sure income

(Isrof qilish yomon odat,

Tejamkorlik yaxshi daromad)

Blushing is a paint of good habits

(Qizarish- yaxshi odatlarning nuqtasi).

Printed by Books on Demand GmbH, Norderstedt / Germany